Edward Burne-J _

Stained Glass in Birmingham Churches

Alastair Carew-Cox   **William Waters**

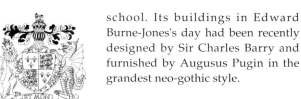

This study of aspects of the work of Edward Burne-Jones is a tribute to him on the centenary of his death. The governers of the ancient foundation of King Edward VI in Birmingham who still preside over Edward Burne-Jones's school are delighted to have been instrumental in the publication of this work and trust it will bring into sharper focus his great achievement, in particular that part of it that is to be found in the churches of Birmingham, his native city.

Most of us, no matter what happens later, owe much to our birth place, our education and particular people we meet in our early years. This was certainly true of Edward Burne-Jones. The Birmingham of his childhood may have been grimy, but it was exciting. Its industrialists were breaking new ground in methods of production and it was the city chosen by John Henry Newman in which to found his oratory after leaving Oxford. As the result of an ancient endowment, it was also a place with a fine school. Its buildings in Edward Burne-Jones's day had been recently designed by Sir Charles Barry and furnished by Augusus Pugin in the grandest neo-gothic style.

Edward Burne-Jones was admitted free to King Edward's School, for his father was rather poor. It was at a propitious time: a new Chief Master, James Prince Lee, was raising it to being one of the leading schools in the country. It was therefore of great importance to the future artist to be born into such a heritage. Nor was it a coincidence that on leaving school he retraced John Henry Newman's footsteps to Oxford. His chosen College was Exeter, the alma mater of the Revd John Goss, a Tractarian clergyman in Birmingham he admired. There he met William Morris. The rest, as they say, is history.

HR Wright
Chief Master
King Edward's School, Birmingham 1998

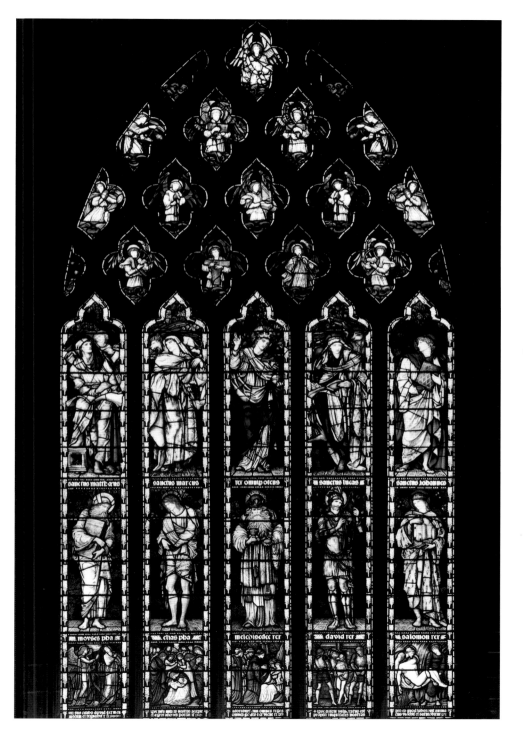

St. Martin's in the Bull Ring

The first stained glass window to be installed within the city of Birmingham from Morris & Co. was the south transept window in the medieval church of St. Martin commissioned in 1876 by Thomas Ryland of Erdington and Moxhul Park, Warwickshire, to commemorate the death of his daughter, Mary. The majority of the large window, which comprises three tiers and tracery, was produced from existing cartoons but three of the designs were made especially for this occasion. These were 'The Entombment' and 'The Flagellation' at the bottom right, and 'Melchisedec' a full length figure in the centre of the second tier. Burne-Jones charged £10 for each of these designs - recorded in his account book (Fitzwilliam Museum). Morris made a rule that he would not place windows in ancient buildings, a rule which coincided with his involvement with the Society for the Preservation of Ancient Buildings. St. Martin's is one of the few exceptions, presumably since the south transept was being renewed at the time.

As an example of middle period Morris & Co. productions this window compares well with any others that were made at this time. It manifests the competence of design, colour and craftsmanship that was their contribution to the Aesthetic movement. The overall control of colour and light is typical of Morris's taste, most notably in his use of white and gold against dark patterned backgrounds of red and blue. The fruit and foliage that decorate areas above the figures have much in common with the wallpaper and fabrics he was making during the 1870s. Perhaps the most interesting of the figures are the four evangelists on either side of 'Christ, Salvator Mundi.' Originally designed for Jesus College Chapel, Cambridge, in 1873, their dynamic forms appear to gyrate and burst from their niches. They overlap their decorative borders in contrast to the figures below and their emblems ingeniously occupy subtle positions upon their shoulders. When they were designed

previous page. St Martin's in the Bull Ring, overall window. A simpler design was discussed at first to include a stock cartoon of The Transfiguration (Morris & Co. sketch design, Wightwick Manor collection). This was rejected in preference for the more complex final design.
above. Solomon, detail. As a background to the figure Morris has used acorns and oak leaves above a Medieval inspired backcloth.
right. Angel with Dulcimer. Heaven is represented as in most Victorian windows by undulating waves of blue.
above right. Moses, Elias and Melchisidec. The original option of using an existing design of The Transfiguration (St. Cuthberts, Lytham 1875) was not totally abandoned as the two figures of Moses and Elias were retained.

moyses pba   **elias pba**   **melchisedec rex**

Burne-Jones had recently returned from a period in Rome, intensely studying Michealangelo's frescos in the Sistine Chapel which explains their massive qualities. In comparison, those figures below in the second tier, are slim and elegant typifying an alternative style he used contemporaneously. Moses and Elias were designed for Lytham (Lancs.) in 1876 and David and Solomon were for Calcutta Cathedral in 1874.

Narrative scenes occupy the lowest tier. 'The Annunciation,' 'The Nativity' and 'The Adoration of the Magi' were first designed for Castle Howard Chapel (Yorks.) in 1872 and because of their popular subject matter were used repeatedly. Usually, when a cartoon is specially commissioned its first use is the best; this is true of 'The Flagellation' and 'The Deposition'. These designs are both ingenious in their use of the space; their energetic lines convey the emotion of the narrative. St. Martin's. being a low church did not include a Crucifixion in the window, substituting 'The Flagellation' to exemplify Christ's suffering for mankind.

The tall, narrow lancets of the Gothic window in St. Martin's Church present a good example of Burne-Jones's habit of designing figures suitable for the space. With considerable ingenuity he adapted his designs, never being predictable even though he had to repeat his subject matter frequently, as the commissions demanded. However, his later work naturally developed a pictorial tendency that was more suited to the larger open spaces created by neo-classical architecture in which other, equally difficult problems arose. How he solved these we shall see in the windows of St.Philip's.

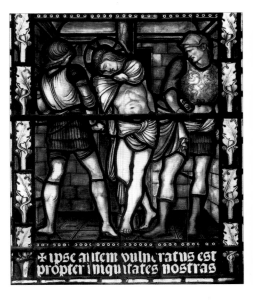

from left to right with translations from the Vulgate for the latin quotations; The Annunciation; 'I shall raise up for David a righteous Branch, and he shall reign as King ...' Jeremiah 23.5. The Nativity; 'He took our infirmities and bore our sicknesses.' Matthew 8.17. It is interesting to note that Matthew evidently refers to Isaiah 53.4 and claims to be quoting Isaiah, but he misquotes to make the verse refer to physical rather than spiritual weakness. The Adoration of the Magi; 'All kings shall adore him, all nations shall serve him.' Psalm 71.11. The Vulgate is quoted with words missing. The Flagellation; 'And he was bruised for our iniquities' Isaiah 53.5.

right. The Entombment; 'He shall see what his soul has laboured for, and be satisfied.' Isaiah 53.11.

Morris and Burne-Jones have deliberately chosen a sombre tonality by using a restricted range of colours, which reflect the mood of The Flagellation and The Entombment. This suggests it was these original subjects that dictated the overall impression of the larger window.

pro eo quod laboravit anima
eius videbit et saturabitur

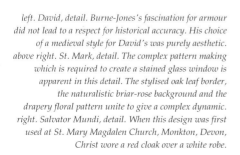

left. David, detail. Burne-Jones's fascination for armour did not lead to a respect for historical accuracy. His choice of a medieval style for David's was purely aesthetic. above right. St. Mark, detail. The complex pattern making which is required to create a stained glass window is apparent in this detail. The stylised oak leaf border, the naturalistic briar-rose background and the drapery floral pattern unite to give a complex dynamic. right. Salvator Mundi, detail. When this design was first used at St. Mary Magdalen Church, Monkton, Devon, Christ wore a red cloak over a white robe.

St. Mary the Virgin, Acocks Green

Situated in the suburb of Acocks Green, J G Bland's Church of 1866 has been much modified owing to severe bomb damage during World War Two. It suffered a direct hit and consequently the majority of the Victorian stained glass was destroyed. Happily Burne-Jone's east window and the magnificent reredos were not. They were removed for safe keeping during the rest of the war and only suffered minor damage before being reinstated. Today window and reredos survive as an integrated unit maintaining the original intention of their respective designers.

The east window showing Christ on the Cross attended by the Virgin Mary and St. John, flanked by two Angels bearing scrolls was installed by Morris & Co. in 1895 as a result of a commission by the widow and son of the Rev. Frederick Thomas Swinburn. None of the figures were specially designed, they were all taken from stock cartoons and re-interpreted. Christ with the Virgin and St. John were originally designed for St. Michael's Church, Torquay in 1877, the Angels with scrolls for All Saint's Church, Ruskington in 1874, the Angels in the tracery for All Hallow's Church, Allerton in 1882 and the Symbols of the Evangelists were designed by Phillip Webb for the Church of St. Michael and All Angels, Lyndhurst in 1861-2.

The window is a tribute both to Burne-Jones's capability as a designer and to John Henry Dearle's skill as chief foreman and craftsman. During the eighteen nineties Dearle took on increasingly the supervision of stained glass production, whilst William Morris and Burne-Jones were absorbed in their other interests, most notably the Kelmscott Press. Under Dearle, late Morris & Co. windows take on their characteristic expressionistic leading and colour.

left. Overall view of Chancel, St. Mary The Virgin, Acocks Green showing alabaster reredos by Bridgman of Lichfield, 1903. above. The Crucifixion. By the use of mosaic leading as a background, the figure of Christ and the foliaceous cross are made more prominent.

17

The scroll text reads:

ET SICVT
MOYSES
EXALTAVIT
SERPENTĒ
IN DESERTO
ITA EXALT-
ARI OPOR-
TET FILIV̄
HOMINIS

above. The Virgin Mary and Angel with Scroll.
Translation of latin text (John 3.14) reads
'Just as Moses lifted up the serpent in the wilderness,
so ought the Son of Man to be lifted up.'
right. Angel with Scroll, detail.
By 1895 JH Dearle's influence on Morris & Co.'s glass was paramount.
The colours shown are typical of those used by him from 1898 to the late 1930's.

INRI

S·MARY

S·JOHN

ET SI CVT
MOYSES
XALTAVIT
ERPENTE
IN DESERTO
TA EXALT
ARI OPOR
TET FILIV
HOMINIS

IN HOC COG
NONIMVS
CHARITA
TEM DEI
QVONIAM
ILLE ANIMA
SVVM PRO
NOBIS POVIT

SIC VS
DILEXIT
MVDVM

E GLORY OF GOD AND IN LOVING   MEMORY OF THE REV. FREDERICK   OF ARCHIS WITH THIS WINDOW WAS   RECTED BY HIS WIFE AND S

Continuing the style initiated by Morris and Burne-Jones, without their genius it has to be said, he creates windows which are competent examples of late nineteenth century stained glass technology which compare favourably with those produced by the emergent Arts and Crafts movement.

The seven strong team that produced the window benefited from over thirty years experience which is manifest in the modelling of the flesh tones, the sensitive selection of colours and the mosaic patterning of the lead lines. The contrast between the figural elements and the pervasive blue sky is made with telling effect, Dearle respected Burne-Jones's preference for a calm, solemn crucifixion by choosing dark tones to accompany the dignity and restraint of the poses. In their original context, the Angels with scrolls stood on either side of a resurrected Christ and if they appear a trifle incongruous in the present setting it demonstrates the flaw of choosing pre-existing figures from stock. Burne-Jones's style had changed between 1877, the date of the Crucifixion and 1882 the date of the Angels, who manifest his taste for neo-classical draperies supplanting his interest in the late Renaissance.

left. Overall window, St. Mary The Virgin.
By the time the windows were installed, Morris & Co. had amassed a huge stock of cartoons from which clients were able to choose. The cartoons used here range from 1861 to 1882.
right. Symbols of the Evangelists, designed by Phillip Webb 1861-2. from top to bottom;
St. Matthew, St. Mark, St. Luke, St. John.

The Cathedral Church of St. Philip

In order to accommodate the growing congregation, St. Philip's church underwent a significant enlargement at the east end in 1884. An opportunity to create three large windows was thus presented utilising an endowment made by Miss Emma Chadwick Villiers-Wilkes for the suitable beautification of a subsequent cathedral church. A natural choice was the firm of Morris & Co. because of William Morris's and Burne-Jones's recent involvement in the artistic activities of the city.

The first stained glass to be installed was the central light and depicted 'The Ascension' (1885) in the newly created space. Two years later, on either side the subjects chosen were 'The Crucifixion' and 'The Nativity.' The artist received £200 for each of his designs, a fact recorded in his account book along with his wry comments:

"For St Philip's Church, Birmingham (my native town) a colossal design of the Ascension; perhaps my fiftieth treatment of this subject - involving much physical fatigue in addition to mental weariness. How inevitably indelicate are all money transactions! Connected now for ever in my memory with this noble theme is a base offer of a flagrantly inadequate sum by way of payment. Was it hoped that in the absorption & rapture of composition I might be exploited unwarily? or because my sympathies were enlisted by the associations of youth was it hoped that I should be satisfied, clothed & fed with the glow of early memories? Is it permitted me to say, that to be swindled in my old age in no way compensates me for the slights of my unappreciated infancy. Take this design then at you (sic) own valuation - the price you fix is the price at which you set your own honour & conscience - & is the measure of that. £200."

and on the next page:

"To first design of same "on approval" (ye gods!) £20."

It is difficult to assess whether such banter covered a genuine grievance, as £200 represented a considerable sum at the time.

left. The Last Judgement, detail.
above. The Nativity. Burne-Jones has returned to his love for medieval art for inspiration in this window. The stark bare trees, the elemental rocks and child like innocence are derived from his intimate knowledge of medieval manuscripts.

For the following Nativity and Crucifixion designs in the side windows his account book also contains these remarks:

"2 cartoons for St Philip's, Birmingham. We come now to an event in the history of my connexion with the firm upon which I would fain have kept silence: as it is I can but implore those who hereafter have curiosity or interest enough to peruse this ledger, to withhold from public notice the disastrous transaction now to be recorded. It was in the year (I was about to say of Grace) 1885 that visiting my native city of Birmingham I was so struck with admiration at one of my works in St Philip's Church - (May I mention parenthetically that in that very church at the tender age of a few weeks I was enlisted amongst the rank and file of the church militant) struck with admiration at my own work (a naive confession which all artists will condone) I undertook in a moment of enthusiasm to fill the windows on either side with compositions which I hoped and perhaps not unreasonably hoped to make worthy of my former achievement..."

Great efforts were made to produce windows worthy of the commission. The Firm's best painters were employed, Bowman and John Henry Dearle, the latter being subsequently in charge of the Firm when Morris and Burne-Jones had died.

There has been much discussion over Burne-Jones's tendency in his later work to create large pictorial windows, to quote a contemporary:

"St Philip's, Birmingham... (presents) a logical outcome of a painter's disposition to make attractive pictures rather than practical working drawings. The inevitable result of discontinuing the systematic practice of showing colour and inserting the lead lines was that however much the designs gained in other ways, they gradually lost in respect of those special characteristics which distinguish glass painting from the rest of the arts."

One feels that the writer cannot have spent much time considering the windows, since the impression they give is one of monumentality in harmony with the architectural space. The images fit their context like an illumination on a medieval manuscript, in fact it would be true to say that the origin of the windows lay within that sphere as will be explained later. The windows are neither subservient to, nor dominate the building but in fact unify with the existing eighteenth century interior to create something entirely new and unique.

These windows show the art of Burne-Jones at its greatest. He utilised traditional images culled from the medieval period onwards for their iconic impact. His use of them however is totally new, seeking to express his deeply felt spirituality through the creation of mood and atmosphere, and like his contemporaries, the Symbolist painters in Europe, his intention is to generate similar feelings in the viewer by means of aesthetic devices. Christ is revealed seated on a rainbow that symbolises the salvation of the souls he portrays in the crepuscular collapsing world below. Not believing in the damnatory and judgmental aspects of the Christian Church, he concentrates on universal salvation and the forgiving aspects of the Christian dogma. The predominant use of warm pinks and strong, assertive colours amplifies this meaning carried by the cartoon. Seen together the three windows combine to impart devotional awe, to quote the artist:

"I couldn't do without medieval Christianity. The central idea of it and all it has gathered to itself made the Europe that I exist in. The enthusiasm and devotion, the learning and

left. The Nativity, detail. Burne-Jones has chosen the traditional manner of representing the Virgin by clothing her in a mantle of blue.

25

At the west end, 'The Last Judgement' displays the pinnacle of Burne-Jones's achievement which claims its place among the masterpieces of stained glass. It was almost the last to be designed, although the sketch was prepared in January 1889. Strangely his accounts show that he only received £70 for the work, this may be because the cartoon was produced through photographic enlargement and therefore did not require as much work. He may also have wanted his masterpiece to be in his home city and thus asked a reduced price.

Paradoxically, this huge design would seem to have its origin in Romanesque illuminated manuscripts. In these are the characteristics that are to be found in Burne-Jones's late style - elongated narrow bodies, small heads in relation to body length and the design which occupies a large space divided into two equal halves horizontally, in which the two groups of figures relate to one another directly, with the central figure superimposed between them. Naked feet of Angels show clear derivation from Romanesque manuscripts for example the twelfth century Psalter of Shaftsbury Abbey (Lansdowne MS 383) which Burne-Jones would have come across on one of his frequent visits to the British museum.

left. The Crucifixion. Reduced to almost mathematical symmetry, Burne-Jones's design has ingeniously set the standards of the soldiers against The Cross as a counterweight, whilst the figures of Mary and Christ eloquently express the tragic story enacted before the viewer.
right. The Ascension. This window along with The Crucifixion and Nativity windows illustrate the high level of workmanship reached by the studio craftsmen. It is recorded that the painters Bowman and Dearle were responsible for all three.

With consummate mastery Burne-Jones commands this enormous work, its design considerably simpler than that of his earlier working of the subject at St. Michael and Mary Magdalene Church, Easthampstead, Berkshire, (1874). In St. Philip's he has deliberately played down the traditional figures rising from the tomb, St. Michael weighing the souls of the dead and any hint of damnation are eliminated. He ingeniously understates catastrophe by means of a central band of shadowy, falling buildings merely using it as a foil for the drama of the trumpeting Angel. Dwarfed by the window, the viewer's gaze is led from the child at the base, up to its mother, across the Angel with trumpet, to Christ in Majesty surrounded by the Chorus Angelorum. In a substantial number of Burne-Jones's late works it is usual for a single figure to engage the onlooker's attention through a direct gaze; this is the purpose of the two figures emerging from the tombs at the base of the composition who involve the active participation of the viewer. In contrast, the windows at the east end demonstrate his method of allowing the viewer only a passive observation of the scenes from the life of Christ. Burne-Jones has chosen that the laity be made to experience wonder at the holy events before them in the east end but as they leave the cathedral they are warned of the Judgement to come, a stratagem which he had derived from medieval tradition that situated the Crucifixion at the east end and the Last Judgement at the west for a similar didactic purpose.

Even when admiration of Burne-Jones as an artist was at its lowest point during World War II, Birmingham demonstrated its deep respect for the cathedral windows. Bishop Barnes, the controversial Bishop of the time, had all of the windows removed when they were under threat of damage by enemy bombing.

Birmingham today acknowledges its artist genius, who a hundred years after his death is recognised as being amongst the greatest of artists in glass. From being one of the Pre-Raphaelite followers who chose to bring the art from out of the neglect of the centuries before, he took it to new heights of expressive power. His skills and example paved the way forward for twentieth century artists to accept stained glass as the major art form that it is today.

above left and above right. The Ascension, details.
The variety of character expressed in the faces of
Mary and the Disciples refutes the often made
claim that all Burne-Jones's faces are similar.

left and far left. The Crucifixion, details. Burne-Jones could not resist including the faces of insensitive Philistine followers in the crowd below The Cross. Uniquely in his output he has portrayed the baser elements of mankind which hitherto had only been found amongst his characatures.

*left. The Last Judgement.
Arguably Burne-Jones's greatest
achievement, greater even than
his paintings. It took five
painter-craftsmen to produce it;
Walters, Bowman, Wren, Stokes
and Titcomb who were continually
supervised by Burne-Jones.
right. The Last Judgement, detail.*